Multiplication

Multiplying Numbers 1 Through 9

P9-CAE-912

Multiplication Speed & Accuracy Log

Practice

	Time	0'00"	1'00"	2'00"	3'00"	4'00"	5'00" Score
13	' "						
14	' "						
15	' "						
16	' "						
17	' "						
18	' "						
19	' "						
20	' "						
21	' "						
22	' "						
23	' "						
24	' "						
25	' "						
26	' "						
27	' "						
28	' "						
29	' "						
30	' "						
31	' "						
32	' "						
33	' "						
34	' "						
35	' "						
36	' "						
37	' "						
38	' "						
39	' "						
40	' "						

Sprint

	Time	0'00"	1'00"	2'00"	3'00"	4'00"	5'00" Score
41	' "						
42	' "						
43	' "						
44	' "						
45	' "						
46	' "						
47	' "						
48	' "						
49	' "						
50	' "						
51	' "						
52	' "						
53	' "						
54	' "						
55	' "						
56	' "						

How to log your results

Write your time and score for each page. Plot your results in the graph with a dot and connect the dots to show your progress.

Example

	Time	0'00"	1'00"	2'00"	3'00"	4'00"	5'00" Score
13	2'30"						45
14	3'30"						38
15	2'33"						43
16	2'40"						40
17	3'00"						37
18	2'30"						45
19	2'10"						

As you work through the book, your progress may vary, but your speed and accuracy will surely improve. Continue to log your time and score to see the positive changes—you may get faster, become more accurate, and/or feel more confident in your skills. Pay close attention to any changes you observe.

Target Time
2 / 3 / 4 min.
* Based on your time from the previous page, circle a target time for completing this page.

Date
/   /

Name

● Multiply.

① 5 × 8 =

② 2 × 9 =

③ 4 × 5 =

④ 3 × 7 =

⑤ 5 × 1 =

⑥ 2 × 6 =

⑦ 3 × 2 =

⑧ 4 × 4 =

⑨ 3 × 6 =

⑩ 5 × 4 =

⑪ 3 × 8 =

⑫ 2 × 2 =

⑬ 5 × 9 =

⑭ 4 × 3 =

⑮ 3 × 5 =

⑯ 5 × 2 =

⑰ 4 × 8 =

⑱ 3 × 1 =

⑲ 5 × 5 =

⑳ 4 × 2 =

㉑ 2 × 8 =

㉒ 4 × 9 =

㉓ 5 × 7 =

㉔ 2 × 1 =

㉕ 3 × 3 =

㉖ 4 × 6 =

㉗ 5 × 3 =

㉘ 3 × 9 =

㉙ 2 × 5 =

㉚ 4 × 7 =

㉛ 2 × 4 =

㉜ 5 × 6 =

㉝ 2 × 7 =

㉞ 4 × 1 =

㉟ 3 × 4 =

㊱ 2 × 3 =

㊲ 5 × 2 =

㊳ 3 × 9 =

㊴ 4 × 4 =

㊵ 2 × 6 =

㊶ 3 × 2 =

㊷ 4 × 7 =

㊸ 3 × 1 =

㊹ 2 × 4 =

㊺ 5 × 6 =

Score

Your Time

min.   sec.

/45

16

Practice

Multiplication from 2× to 5×

Target Time
2 / 3 / 4 min.
* Based on your time from the previous page, circle a target time for completing this page.

Date / / **Name**

● Multiply.

① 2 × 2 =

② 4 × 7 =

③ 5 × 5 =

④ 2 × 9 =

⑤ 3 × 2 =

⑥ 4 × 5 =

⑦ 5 × 7 =

⑧ 2 × 6 =

⑨ 5 × 8 =

⑩ 3 × 3 =

⑪ 4 × 4 =

⑫ 3 × 8 =

⑬ 5 × 9 =

⑭ 2 × 1 =

⑮ 5 × 4 =

⑯ 3 × 9 =

⑰ 2 × 3 =

⑱ 5 × 1 =

⑲ 3 × 4 =

⑳ 4 × 2 =

㉑ 2 × 8 =

㉒ 3 × 1 =

㉓ 4 × 9 =

㉔ 5 × 6 =

㉕ 2 × 5 =

㉖ 4 × 3 =

㉗ 3 × 5 =

㉘ 5 × 2 =

㉙ 2 × 7 =

㉚ 4 × 6 =

㉛ 5 × 3 =

㉜ 3 × 7 =

㉝ 4 × 1 =

㉞ 2 × 4 =

㉟ 3 × 6 =

㊱ 4 × 8 =

㊲ 5 × 1 =

㊳ 3 × 4 =

㊴ 2 × 8 =

㊵ 4 × 6 =

㊶ 5 × 7 =

㊷ 2 × 5 =

㊸ 4 × 3 =

㊹ 3 × 6 =

㊺ 2 × 2 =

Your Time min. sec.

Score /45

17

Target Time

2 / 3 / 4 min.

* Based on your time from the previous page, circle a target time for completing this page.

Date / /

Name

● Mu

① 3 ×

② 4 × 2 =

③ 5 × 6 =

④ 3 × 3 =

⑤ 2 × 5 =

⑥ 4 × 6 =

⑦ 5 × 2 =

⑧ 3 × 5 =

⑨ 2 × 3 =

⑩ 5 × 7 =

⑪ 4 × 5 =

⑫ 3 × 2 =

⑬ 2 × 8 =

⑭ 5 × 5 =

⑮ 4 × 3 =

⑯ 3 × 1 =

⑰ 5 × 8 =

⑱ × 9 =

⑳ =

㉑ 5

㉒ 2 × 4

㉓ 4 × 7 =

㉔ 3 × 6 =

㉕ 2 × 2 =

㉖ 5 × 3 =

㉗ 4 × 8 =

㉘ 3 × 4 =

㉙ 5 × 9 =

㉚ 2 × 1 =

㉛ 4 × 4 =

㉜ 3 × 8 =

㉝ 5 × 4 =

㉞ 2 × 7 =

㉟ 4 × 1 =

㊱ 2 × 9 =

㊲ 3 × 2 =

㊳ 5 × 7 =

× 7 =

2 =

=

㊷ 5 ×

㊸ 2 × 3

㊹ 4 × 6 =

㊺ 3 × 8 =

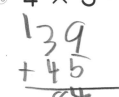

Your Time

min.   sec.

Score

/45

18

Practice
Multiplication from 2× to 5×

Target Time
2 / 3 / 4 min.
* Based on your time from the previous page, circle a target time for completing this page.

Date   /   /   Name

● **Multiply.**

① 4 × 1 =

② 2 × 7 =

③ 3 × 4 =

④ 5 × 7 =

⑤ 4 × 5 =

⑥ 2 × 3 =

⑦ 3 × 7 =

⑧ 5 × 1 =

⑨ 4 × 9 =

⑩ 3 × 2 =

⑪ 2 × 5 =

⑫ 5 × 8 =

⑬ 4 × 7 =

⑭ 2 × 2 =

⑮ 5 × 9 =

⑯ 3 × 8 =

⑰ 4 × 3 =

⑱ 3 × 5 =

⑲ 2 × 6 =

⑳ 5 × 2 =

㉑ 4 × 6 =

㉒ 2 × 9 =

㉓ 3 × 1 =

㉔ 5 × 5 =

㉕ 4 × 8 =

㉖ 2 × 1 =

㉗ 3 × 6 =

㉘ 5 × 3 =

㉙ 4 × 4 =

㉚ 2 × 8 =

㉛ 3 × 9 =

㉜ 5 × 4 =

㉝ 4 × 2 =

㉞ 5 × 6 =

㉟ 2 × 4 =

㊱ 3 × 3 =

㊲ 4 × 8 =

㊳ 5 × 2 =

㊴ 3 × 7 =

㊵ 2 × 2 =

㊶ 4 × 5 =

㊷ 5 × 8 =

㊸ 3 × 4 =

㊹ 2 × 9 =

㊺ 4 × 1 =

Your Time   min.   sec.

Score   /45

Practice
Multiplication from 2× to 5×

Target Time
2 / 3 / 4 min.
* Based on your time from the previous page, circle a target time for completing this page.

Date / /

Name

● **Multiply.**

① 5 × 5 =

② 4 × 8 =

③ 2 × 1 =

④ 3 × 4 =

⑤ 5 × 3 =

⑥ 4 × 6 =

⑦ 2 × 5 =

⑧ 3 × 9 =

⑨ 4 × 3 =

⑩ 5 × 8 =

⑪ 3 × 5 =

⑫ 2 × 2 =

⑬ 4 × 7 =

⑭ 5 × 1 =

⑮ 3 × 6 =

⑯ 4 × 2 =

⑰ 2 × 6 =

⑱ 5 × 7 =

⑲ 3 × 2 =

⑳ 4 × 5 =

㉑ 3 × 8 =

㉒ 5 × 4 =

㉓ 2 × 8 =

㉔ 3 × 3 =

㉕ 4 × 1 =

㉖ 5 × 9 =

㉗ 2 × 3 =

㉘ 4 × 4 =

㉙ 2 × 7 =

㉚ 5 × 2 =

㉛ 3 × 7 =

㉜ 2 × 4 =

㉝ 4 × 9 =

㉞ 5 × 6 =

㉟ 3 × 1 =

㊱ 2 × 9 =

㊲ 4 × 4 =

㊳ 5 × 3 =

㊴ 2 × 6 =

㊵ 4 × 7 =

㊶ 2 × 5 =

㊷ 3 × 3 =

㊸ 5 × 5 =

㊹ 2 × 1 =

㊺ 3 × 9 =

Your Time

min.   sec.

Score

/45

Target Time

2 / 3 / 4 min.

* Based on your time from the previous page, circle a target time for completing this page.

Date

/   /

Name

● **Multiply.**

① 2 × 3 =

② 5 × 8 =

③ 4 × 1 =

④ 3 × 2 =

⑤ 2 × 6 =

⑥ 4 × 4 =

⑦ 5 × 1 =

⑧ 3 × 8 =

⑨ 2 × 9 =

⑩ 5 × 4 =

⑪ 4 × 7 =

⑫ 3 × 6 =

⑬ 2 × 2 =

⑭ 4 × 8 =

⑮ 5 × 5 =

⑯ 3 × 7 =

⑰ 2 × 5 =

⑱ 4 × 3 =

⑲ 5 × 9 =

⑳ 3 × 1 =

㉑ 2 × 8 =

㉒ 5 × 2 =

㉓ 3 × 5 =

㉔ 4 × 9 =

㉕ 2 × 1 =

㉖ 3 × 4 =

㉗ 4 × 6 =

㉘ 5 × 3 =

㉙ 3 × 9 =

㉚ 2 × 4 =

㉛ 5 × 7 =

㉜ 4 × 5 =

㉝ 3 × 3 =

㉞ 2 × 7 =

㉟ 4 × 2 =

㊱ 5 × 6 =

㊲ 3 × 1 =

㊳ 2 × 8 =

㊴ 5 × 4 =

㊵ 4 × 9 =

㊶ 3 × 6 =

㊷ 5 × 9 =

㊸ 2 × 4 =

㊹ 4 × 3 =

㊺ 5 × 6 =

Your Time

min.   sec.

Score

.

/45

Practice
Multiplication from 2× to 5×

Target Time

2 / 3 / 4 min.

* Based on your time from the previous page, circle a target time for completing this page.

Date

/   /

Name

● **Multiply.**

① $3 \times 2 =$

② $2 \times 8 =$

③ $4 \times 2 =$

④ $5 \times 1 =$

⑤ $3 \times 9 =$

⑥ $5 \times 5 =$

⑦ $4 \times 8 =$

⑧ $2 \times 3 =$

⑨ $3 \times 7 =$

⑩ $4 \times 4 =$

⑪ $2 \times 2 =$

⑫ $5 \times 8 =$

⑬ $3 \times 4 =$

⑭ $4 \times 7 =$

⑮ $2 \times 6 =$

⑯ $5 \times 4 =$

⑰ $3 \times 8 =$

⑱ $4 \times 6 =$

⑲ $2 \times 1 =$

⑳ $5 \times 6 =$

㉑ $3 \times 5 =$

㉒ $4 \times 1 =$

㉓ $2 \times 9 =$

㉔ $5 \times 2 =$

㉕ $4 \times 9 =$

㉖ $3 \times 1 =$

㉗ $2 \times 7 =$

㉘ $4 \times 5 =$

㉙ $5 \times 3 =$

㉚ $3 \times 6 =$

㉛ $4 \times 3 =$

㉜ $2 \times 4 =$

㉝ $5 \times 9 =$

㉞ $3 \times 3 =$

㉟ $5 \times 7 =$

㊱ $2 \times 5 =$

㊲ $4 \times 1 =$

㊳ $3 \times 4 =$

㊴ $2 \times 9 =$

㊵ $5 \times 3 =$

㊶ $4 \times 5 =$

㊷ $3 \times 7 =$

㊸ $2 \times 3 =$

㊹ $5 \times 2 =$

㊺ $4 \times 8 =$

Score

Your Time

min.   sec.

/45

Practice
Multiplication from 2× to 5×

Target Time

2 / 3 / 4 min.

* Based on your time from the previous page,
circle a target time for completing this page.

Date

/ /

Name

● **Multiply.**

① 4 × 9 =

② 5 × 7 =

③ 2 × 2 =

④ 3 × 8 =

⑤ 4 × 6 =

⑥ 5 × 4 =

⑦ 2 × 8 =

⑧ 3 × 5 =

⑨ 4 × 3 =

⑩ 3 × 1 =

⑪ 5 × 8 =

⑫ 2 × 1 =

⑬ 4 × 7 =

⑭ 5 × 2 =

⑮ 2 × 9 =

⑯ 3 × 4 =

⑰ 4 × 1 =

⑱ 5 × 6 =

⑲ 2 × 5 =

⑳ 3 × 7 =

㉑ 5 × 1 =

㉒ 4 × 4 =

㉓ 2 × 7 =

㉔ 5 × 5 =

㉕ 3 × 2 =

㉖ 4 × 8 =

㉗ 2 × 4 =

㉘ 3 × 9 =

㉙ 5 × 3 =

㉚ 4 × 5 =

㉛ 3 × 3 =

㉜ 2 × 6 =

㉝ 4 × 2 =

㉞ 3 × 6 =

㉟ 5 × 9 =

㊱ 2 × 3 =

㊲ 5 × 1 =

㊳ 4 × 7 =

㊴ 3 × 2 =

㊵ 2 × 8 =

㊶ 5 × 6 =

㊷ 3 × 9 =

㊸ 4 × 3 =

㊹ 2 × 2 =

㊺ 5 × 4 =

Your Time

min.   sec.

Score

/45

Practice
Multiplication from 2× to 5×

Target Time

2 / **3** / **4** min.

* Based on your time from the previous page, circle a target time for completing this page.

Date   /   /

Name

● **Multiply.**

① 5 × 7 =

② 3 × 2 =

③ 4 × 8 =

④ 2 × 1 =

⑤ 5 × 9 =

⑥ 3 × 4 =

⑦ 4 × 5 =

⑧ 2 × 2 =

⑨ 3 × 8 =

⑩ 5 × 1 =

⑪ 4 × 3 =

⑫ 2 × 7 =

⑬ 3 × 6 =

⑭ 5 × 4 =

⑮ 2 × 6 =

⑯ 3 × 1 =

⑰ 4 × 4 =

⑱ 5 × 2 =

⑲ 3 × 7 =

⑳ 2 × 3 =

㉑ 4 × 7 =

㉒ 5 × 6 =

㉓ 2 × 8 =

㉔ 3 × 3 =

㉕ 4 × 6 =

㉖ 5 × 8 =

㉗ 2 × 9 =

㉘ 4 × 2 =

㉙ 3 × 5 =

㉚ 5 × 3 =

㉛ 2 × 5 =

㉜ 3 × 9 =

㉝ 4 × 1 =

㉞ 5 × 5 =

㉟ 4 × 9 =

㊱ 2 × 4 =

㊲ 3 × 3 =

㊳ 5 × 9 =

㊴ 4 × 6 =

㊵ 2 × 6 =

㊶ 3 × 5 =

㊷ 5 × 7 =

㊸ 4 × 4 =

㊹ 2 × 1 =

㊺ 3 × 8 =

Your Time

min.   sec.

Score

/45

Target Time

2 / 3 / 4 min.

*Based on your time from the previous page, circle a target time for completing this page.

Date / /

Name

● Multiply.

① 2 × 8 =

② 3 × 4 =

③ 4 × 1 =

④ 5 × 3 =

⑤ 2 × 6 =

⑥ 4 × 8 =

⑦ 3 × 2 =

⑧ 5 × 5 =

⑨ 2 × 3 =

⑩ 5 × 8 =

⑪ 3 × 9 =

⑫ 4 × 3 =

⑬ 2 × 7 =

⑭ 3 × 3 =

⑮ 5 × 6 =

⑯ 4 × 5 =

⑰ 2 × 2 =

⑱ 5 × 4 =

⑲ 3 × 7 =

⑳ 4 × 2 =

㉑ 2 × 4 =

㉒ 5 × 7 =

㉓ 3 × 1 =

㉔ 4 × 6 =

㉕ 2 × 5 =

㉖ 5 × 1 =

㉗ 3 × 6 =

㉘ 4 × 9 =

㉙ 2 × 1 =

㉚ 3 × 5 =

㉛ 4 × 7 =

㉜ 5 × 2 =

㉝ 2 × 9 =

㉞ 4 × 4 =

㉟ 3 × 8 =

㊱ 5 × 9 =

㊲ 2 × 4 =

㊳ 4 × 2 =

㊴ 3 × 6 =

㊵ 5 × 5 =

㊶ 2 × 7 =

㊷ 4 × 9 =

㊸ 3 × 1 =

㊹ 5 × 8 =

㊺ 2 × 5 =

Your Time

min. sec.

Score

/45

Practice
Multiplication from 2× to 5×

Target Time

2 / 3 / 4 min.

* Based on your time from the previous page, circle a target time for completing this page.

Date   Name

/   /

● **Multiply.**

① 3 × 4 =

② 5 × 8 =

③ 2 × 4 =

④ 4 × 1 =

⑤ 2 × 9 =

⑥ 3 × 7 =

⑦ 5 × 2 =

⑧ 2 × 5 =

⑨ 4 × 8 =

⑩ 3 × 1 =

⑪ 2 × 3 =

⑫ 5 × 7 =

⑬ 4 × 2 =

⑭ 3 × 3 =

⑮ 2 × 7 =

⑯ 5 × 5 =

⑰ 4 × 3 =

⑱ 3 × 8 =

⑲ 2 × 1 =

⑳ 5 × 3 =

㉑ 4 × 9 =

㉒ 3 × 6 =

㉓ 4 × 5 =

㉔ 5 × 9 =

㉕ 2 × 6 =

㉖ 3 × 5 =

㉗ 5 × 1 =

㉘ 2 × 2 =

㉙ 4 × 4 =

㉚ 3 × 9 =

㉛ 4 × 7 =

㉜ 5 × 6 =

㉝ 2 × 8 =

㉞ 3 × 2 =

㉟ 4 × 6 =

㊱ 5 × 4 =

㊲ 2 × 1 =

㊳ 4 × 5 =

㊴ 3 × 8 =

㊵ 5 × 3 =

㊶ 2 × 6 =

㊷ 3 × 1 =

㊸ 4 × 9 =

㊹ 5 × 7 =

㊺ 3 × 5 =

Your Time

min.   sec.

Score

/45

Practice
Multiplication from 2× to 5×

Target Time

2 / 3 / 4 min.

* Based on your time from the previous page, circle a target time for completing this page.

Date / /

Name

● **Multiply.**

① 4 × 7 =

② 2 × 3 =

③ 5 × 5 =

④ 3 × 3 =

⑤ 4 × 9 =

⑥ 5 × 2 =

⑦ 2 × 8 =

⑧ 3 × 4 =

⑨ 4 × 2 =

⑩ 5 × 7 =

⑪ 2 × 6 =

⑫ 3 × 9 =

⑬ 4 × 4 =

⑭ 2 × 1 =

⑮ 3 × 6 =

⑯ 5 × 4 =

⑰ 4 × 6 =

⑱ 5 × 8 =

⑲ 3 × 2 =

⑳ 2 × 9 =

㉑ 4 × 1 =

㉒ 3 × 7 =

㉓ 2 × 4 =

㉔ 5 × 6 =

㉕ 4 × 5 =

㉖ 5 × 1 =

㉗ 3 × 5 =

㉘ 2 × 2 =

㉙ 4 × 3 =

㉚ 3 × 8 =

㉛ 5 × 9 =

㉜ 2 × 7 =

㉝ 5 × 3 =

㉞ 4 × 8 =

㉟ 3 × 1 =

㊱ 2 × 5 =

㊲ 5 × 5 =

㊳ 3 × 6 =

㊴ 4 × 2 =

㊵ 2 × 8 =

㊶ 5 × 1 =

㊷ 3 × 7 =

㊸ 2 × 3 =

㊹ 4 × 6 =

㊺ 5 × 4 =

Your Time

min.   sec.

Score

/45

Practice
Multiplication from 6× to 9×, 1×

Target Time

2 / 3 / 4 min.

* Based on your time from the previous page,
circle a target time for completing this page.

Date
/   /

Name

● **Multiply.**

① 6 × 7 = 42

② 8 × 2 = 16

③ 9 × 9 =

④ 7 × 5 =

⑤ 1 × 7 =

⑥ 6 × 3 =

⑦ 8 × 8 =

⑧ 9 × 1 =

⑨ 7 × 4 =

⑩ 1 × 8 =

⑪ 6 × 5 =

⑫ 8 × 3 =

⑬ 9 × 6 =

⑭ 7 × 9 =

⑮ 6 × 2 =

⑯ 9 × 7 =

⑰ 1 × 1 =

⑱ 7 × 7 =

⑲ 9 × 5 =

⑳ 6 × 9 =

㉑ 8 × 4 =

㉒ 7 × 1 =

㉓ 1 × 5 =

㉔ 9 × 2 =

㉕ 6 × 4 =

㉖ 7 × 8 =

㉗ 8 × 5 =

㉘ 9 × 8 =

㉙ 1 × 2 =

㉚ 8 × 9 =

㉛ 6 × 1 =

㉜ 7 × 3 =

㉝ 1 × 6 =

㉞ 8 × 7 =

㉟ 9 × 4 =

㊱ 6 × 8 =

㊲ 1 × 3 =

㊳ 8 × 1 =

㊴ 7 × 6 =

㊵ 1 × 9 =

㊶ 6 × 6 =

㊷ 9 × 3 =

㊸ 8 × 6 =

㊹ 7 × 2 =

㊺ 1 × 4 =

Score

Your Time

min.   sec.

/45

Practice
Multiplication from 6× to 9×, 1×

Target Time
2 / 3 / 4 min.
* Based on your time from the previous page,
circle a target time for completing this page.

Date / /

Name

● **Multiply.**

① 7 × 2 =

② 9 × 6 =

③ 8 × 1 =

④ 1 × 9 =

⑤ 6 × 4 =

⑥ 7 × 7 =

⑦ 9 × 2 =

⑧ 6 × 1 =

⑨ 1 × 3 =

⑩ 8 × 7 =

⑪ 9 × 5 =

⑫ 7 × 4 =

⑬ 1 × 8 =

⑭ 9 × 7 =

⑮ 8 × 2 =

⑯ 6 × 8 =

⑰ 7 × 5 =

⑱ 9 × 8 =

⑲ 8 × 3 =

⑳ 1 × 4 =

㉑ 6 × 2 =

㉒ 7 × 8 =

㉓ 9 × 4 =

㉔ 8 × 6 =

㉕ 6 × 9 =

㉖ 1 × 1 =

㉗ 7 × 3 =

㉘ 6 × 5 =

㉙ 8 × 9 =

㉚ 1 × 5 =

㉛ 9 × 9 =

㉜ 7 × 6 =

㉝ 8 × 5 =

㉞ 1 × 2 =

㉟ 6 × 7 =

㊱ 9 × 1 =

㊲ 7 × 9 =

㊳ 6 × 3 =

㊴ 8 × 8 =

㊵ 1 × 6 =

㊶ 7 × 1 =

㊷ 8 × 4 =

㊸ 9 × 3 =

㊹ 1 × 7 =

㊺ 6 × 6 =

Score

Your Time

min.   sec.

/45

29

Practice
Multiplication from 6× to 9×, 1×

Target Time

2 / 3 / 4 min.

* Based on your time from the previous page, circle a target time for completing this page.

Date   /   /

Name

● **Multiply.**

① 8 × 9 =

② 9 × 1 =

③ 7 × 7 =

④ 6 × 2 =

⑤ 8 × 6 =

⑥ 9 × 7 =

⑦ 7 × 1 =

⑧ 1 × 2 =

⑨ 6 × 8 =

⑩ 9 × 3 =

⑪ 8 × 2 =

⑫ 1 × 9 =

⑬ 7 × 6 =

⑭ 9 × 5 =

⑮ 6 × 9 =

⑯ 8 × 4 =

⑰ 1 × 6 =

⑱ 9 × 2 =

⑲ 7 × 5 =

⑳ 6 × 3 =

㉑ 8 × 8 =

㉒ 1 × 4 =

㉓ 6 × 7 =

㉔ 7 × 9 =

㉕ 9 × 4 =

㉖ 8 × 1 =

㉗ 1 × 3 =

㉘ 6 × 6 =

㉙ 9 × 9 =

㉚ 7 × 4 =

㉛ 8 × 5 =

㉜ 1 × 8 =

㉝ 7 × 3 =

㉞ 9 × 6 =

㉟ 6 × 4 =

㊱ 8 × 3 =

㊲ 1 × 7 =

㊳ 7 × 8 =

㊴ 6 × 1 =

㊵ 1 × 5 =

㊶ 8 × 7 =

㊷ 7 × 2 =

㊸ 9 × 8 =

㊹ 1 × 1 =

㊺ 6 × 5 =

Score

Your Time

min.   sec.   / 45

Practice
Multiplication from 6× to 9×, 1×

Target Time

2 / 3 / 4 min.
* Based on your time from the previous page, circle a target time for completing this page.

Date / /

Name

● **Multiply.**

① 9 × 5 =

② 1 × 3 =

③ 7 × 1 =

④ 6 × 9 =

⑤ 8 × 7 =

⑥ 9 × 3 =

⑦ 1 × 7 =

⑧ 8 × 6 =

⑨ 7 × 5 =

⑩ 6 × 2 =

⑪ 9 × 9 =

⑫ 7 × 3 =

⑬ 1 × 8 =

⑭ 8 × 2 =

⑮ 6 × 5 =

⑯ 9 × 2 =

⑰ 7 × 4 =

⑱ 6 × 8 =

⑲ 8 × 5 =

⑳ 1 × 2 =

㉑ 9 × 7 =

㉒ 6 × 3 =

㉓ 8 × 1 =

㉔ 1 × 4 =

㉕ 7 × 6 =

㉖ 9 × 4 =

㉗ 8 × 8 =

㉘ 6 × 4 =

㉙ 1 × 9 =

㉚ 7 × 7 =

㉛ 9 × 8 =

㉜ 1 × 1 =

㉝ 8 × 4 =

㉞ 7 × 8 =

㉟ 6 × 1 =

㊱ 9 × 6 =

㊲ 1 × 5 =

㊳ 7 × 2 =

㊴ 8 × 9 =

㊵ 6 × 6 =

㊶ 9 × 1 =

㊷ 1 × 6 =

㊸ 8 × 3 =

㊹ 6 × 7 =

㊺ 7 × 9 =

Your Time

min. sec.

Score

/45

Practice
Multiplication from 6× to 9×, 1×

Target Time

2 / 3 / 4 min.

* Based on your time from the previous page, circle a target time for completing this page.

Date   /   /

Name

● Multiply.

① 1 × 6 =

② 8 × 8 =

③ 6 × 1 =

④ 7 × 5 =

⑤ 9 × 7 =

⑥ 1 × 8 =

⑦ 7 × 2 =

⑧ 9 × 9 =

⑨ 8 × 4 =

⑩ 6 × 8 =

⑪ 9 × 3 =

⑫ 1 × 2 =

⑬ 8 × 7 =

⑭ 7 × 6 =

⑮ 9 × 8 =

⑯ 6 × 4 =

⑰ 1 × 5 =

⑱ 8 × 9 =

⑲ 9 × 2 =

⑳ 7 × 7 =

㉑ 1 × 1 =

㉒ 6 × 9 =

㉓ 8 × 5 =

㉔ 7 × 3 =

㉕ 6 × 7 =

㉖ 1 × 4 =

㉗ 9 × 6 =

㉘ 8 × 1 =

㉙ 6 × 3 =

㉚ 7 × 4 =

㉛ 1 × 7 =

㉜ 7 × 9 =

㉝ 9 × 5 =

㉞ 8 × 3 =

㉟ 6 × 2 =

㊱ 1 × 9 =

㊲ 9 × 4 =

㊳ 6 × 6 =

㊴ 7 × 1 =

㊵ 8 × 6 =

㊶ 1 × 3 =

㊷ 6 × 5 =

㊸ 9 × 1 =

㊹ 7 × 8 =

㊺ 8 × 2 =

Your Time

min.   sec.

Score

/45

Practice
Multiplication from 6× to 9×, 1×

Target Time

2 / 3 / 4 min.

* Based on your time from the previous page,
circle a target time for completing this page.

Date   /   /

Name

● **Multiply.**

① 6 × 4 =

② 1 × 5 =

③ 8 × 9 =

④ 7 × 3 =

⑤ 9 × 6 =

⑥ 1 × 2 =

⑦ 6 × 9 =

⑧ 8 × 4 =

⑨ 1 × 8 =

⑩ 9 × 3 =

⑪ 6 × 7 =

⑫ 7 × 5 =

⑬ 9 × 8 =

⑭ 8 × 2 =

⑮ 1 × 3 =

⑯ 6 × 6 =

⑰ 9 × 1 =

⑱ 7 × 9 =

⑲ 8 × 5 =

⑳ 1 × 9 =

㉑ 6 × 2 =

㉒ 8 × 1 =

㉓ 9 × 5 =

㉔ 7 × 4 =

㉕ 1 × 7 =

㉖ 6 × 5 =

㉗ 9 × 9 =

㉘ 7 × 1 =

㉙ 8 × 8 =

㉚ 1 × 4 =

㉛ 6 × 1 =

㉜ 9 × 7 =

㉝ 8 × 6 =

㉞ 7 × 8 =

㉟ 1 × 6 =

㊱ 6 × 3 =

㊲ 7 × 6 =

㊳ 9 × 2 =

㊴ 8 × 7 =

㊵ 7 × 2 =

㊶ 6 × 8 =

㊷ 1 × 1 =

㊸ 8 × 3 =

㊹ 9 × 4 =

㊺ 7 × 7 =

Your Time   min.   sec.

Score

/45

Practice
Multiplication from 6× to 9×, 1×

Target Time

2 / 3 / 4 min.

* Based on your time from the previous page, circle a target time for completing this page.

Date   /   /

Name

● **Multiply.**

① 7 × 9 =

② 9 × 1 =

③ 8 × 6 =

④ 1 × 3 =

⑤ 6 × 8 =

⑥ 7 × 2 =

⑦ 1 × 6 =

⑧ 8 × 8 =

⑨ 6 × 1 =

⑩ 9 × 5 =

⑪ 7 × 4 =

⑫ 1 × 7 =

⑬ 8 × 5 =

⑭ 9 × 7 =

⑮ 6 × 6 =

⑯ 7 × 7 =

⑰ 1 × 1 =

⑱ 6 × 3 =

⑲ 9 × 4 =

⑳ 8 × 2 =

㉑ 7 × 5 =

㉒ 6 × 9 =

㉓ 1 × 4 =

㉔ 8 × 3 =

㉕ 9 × 9 =

㉖ 7 × 1 =

㉗ 9 × 3 =

㉘ 1 × 8 =

㉙ 8 × 7 =

㉚ 6 × 2 =

㉛ 7 × 6 =

㉜ 9 × 8 =

㉝ 6 × 4 =

㉞ 8 × 9 =

㉟ 1 × 5 =

㊱ 7 × 3 =

㊲ 9 × 6 =

㊳ 8 × 1 =

㊴ 1 × 9 =

㊵ 6 × 5 =

㊶ 7 × 8 =

㊷ 1 × 2 =

㊸ 8 × 4 =

㊹ 6 × 7 =

㊺ 9 × 2 =

Score

Your Time

min.   sec.

/45

Practice
Multiplication from 6× to 9×, 1×

Target Time

2 / 3 / 4 min.

* Based on your time from the previous page, circle a target time for completing this page.

Date / /

Name

● **Multiply.**

① 8 × 1 =

② 9 × 9 =

③ 6 × 6 =

④ 7 × 4 =

⑤ 1 × 7 =

⑥ 8 × 3 =

⑦ 9 × 5 =

⑧ 7 × 6 =

⑨ 1 × 9 =

⑩ 6 × 1 =

⑪ 8 × 7 =

⑫ 9 × 3 =

⑬ 6 × 8 =

⑭ 1 × 2 =

⑮ 7 × 5 =

⑯ 9 × 1 =

⑰ 8 × 4 =

⑱ 7 × 7 =

⑲ 1 × 5 =

⑳ 6 × 2 =

㉑ 9 × 4 =

㉒ 8 × 8 =

㉓ 6 × 9 =

㉔ 9 × 7 =

㉕ 1 × 4 =

㉖ 7 × 3 =

㉗ 8 × 6 =

㉘ 9 × 2 =

㉙ 6 × 7 =

㉚ 1 × 3 =

㉛ 7 × 8 =

㉜ 8 × 2 =

㉝ 9 × 6 =

㉞ 6 × 5 =

㉟ 1 × 8 =

㊱ 7 × 1 =

㊲ 8 × 9 =

㊳ 6 × 3 =

㊴ 1 × 6 =

㊵ 7 × 2 =

㊶ 9 × 8 =

㊷ 8 × 5 =

㊸ 1 × 1 =

㊹ 7 × 9 =

㊺ 6 × 4 =

Score

Your Time

min.   sec.

/45

Target Time

2 / 3 / 4 min.

* Based on your time from the previous page, circle a target time for completing this page.

Date   /   /

Name

● **Multiply.**

① 9 × 3 =

② 1 × 7 =

③ 7 × 9 =

④ 8 × 1 =

⑤ 6 × 2 =

⑥ 1 × 9 =

⑦ 9 × 4 =

⑧ 8 × 8 =

⑨ 7 × 6 =

⑩ 1 × 2 =

⑪ 6 × 8 =

⑫ 9 × 9 =

⑬ 7 × 7 =

⑭ 8 × 3 =

⑮ 1 × 8 =

⑯ 6 × 5 =

⑰ 9 × 1 =

⑱ 1 × 5 =

⑲ 8 × 4 =

⑳ 7 × 2 =

㉑ 6 × 6 =

㉒ 9 × 7 =

㉓ 1 × 1 =

㉔ 8 × 9 =

㉕ 7 × 8 =

㉖ 6 × 3 =

㉗ 9 × 5 =

㉘ 8 × 2 =

㉙ 7 × 3 =

㉚ 1 × 6 =

㉛ 9 × 8 =

㉜ 8 × 7 =

㉝ 7 × 5 =

㉞ 1 × 4 =

㉟ 6 × 1 =

㊱ 9 × 2 =

㊲ 8 × 5 =

㊳ 6 × 7 =

㊴ 7 × 4 =

㊵ 6 × 9 =

㊶ 9 × 6 =

㊷ 1 × 3 =

㊸ 8 × 6 =

㊹ 6 × 4 =

㊺ 7 × 1 =

Your Time

min.   sec.

Score

/45

Practice
Multiplication from 6× to 9×, 1×

Target Time

2 / 3 / 4 min.

* Based on your time from the previous page, circle a target time for completing this page.

Date   /   /

Name

● **Multiply.**

① 1 × 8 =

② 8 × 4 =

③ 9 × 6 =

④ 7 × 5 =

⑤ 6 × 8 =

⑥ 1 × 3 =

⑦ 9 × 1 =

⑧ 7 × 7 =

⑨ 6 × 2 =

⑩ 8 × 8 =

⑪ 1 × 6 =

⑫ 9 × 9 =

⑬ 8 × 2 =

⑭ 6 × 4 =

⑮ 7 × 3 =

⑯ 1 × 1 =

⑰ 8 × 9 =

⑱ 7 × 6 =

⑲ 9 × 2 =

⑳ 1 × 7 =

㉑ 6 × 3 =

㉒ 7 × 9 =

㉓ 8 × 5 =

㉔ 9 × 8 =

㉕ 1 × 4 =

㉖ 6 × 6 =

㉗ 7 × 2 =

㉘ 9 × 5 =

㉙ 8 × 7 =

㉚ 1 × 9 =

㉛ 8 × 3 =

㉜ 9 × 4 =

㉝ 6 × 9 =

㉞ 8 × 1 =

㉟ 7 × 4 =

㊱ 1 × 2 =

㊲ 6 × 5 =

㊳ 9 × 7 =

㊴ 6 × 1 =

㊵ 7 × 8 =

㊶ 1 × 5 =

㊷ 6 × 7 =

㊸ 9 × 3 =

㊹ 7 × 1 =

㊺ 8 × 6 =

Your Time

min.   sec.

Score

/45

Target Time

2 / 3 / 4 min.

* Based on your time from the previous page, circle a target time for completing this page.

Date / /

Name

● **Multiply.**

① $6 \times 1 =$

② $9 \times 4 =$

③ $8 \times 3 =$

④ $7 \times 6 =$

⑤ $1 \times 9 =$

⑥ $6 \times 4 =$

⑦ $8 \times 6 =$

⑧ $9 \times 8 =$

⑨ $7 \times 7 =$

⑩ $1 \times 3 =$

⑪ $6 \times 8 =$

⑫ $9 \times 2 =$

⑬ $1 \times 6 =$

⑭ $8 \times 5 =$

⑮ $7 \times 9 =$

⑯ $8 \times 8 =$

⑰ $6 \times 5 =$

⑱ $1 \times 8 =$

⑲ $7 \times 1 =$

⑳ $9 \times 3 =$

㉑ $8 \times 9 =$

㉒ $6 \times 7 =$

㉓ $1 \times 2 =$

㉔ $7 \times 5 =$

㉕ $9 \times 7 =$

㉖ $6 \times 9 =$

㉗ $8 \times 4 =$

㉘ $9 \times 9 =$

㉙ $1 \times 5 =$

㉚ $7 \times 2 =$

㉛ $6 \times 3 =$

㉜ $7 \times 4 =$

㉝ $9 \times 1 =$

㉞ $1 \times 7 =$

㉟ $8 \times 2 =$

㊱ $6 \times 6 =$

㊲ $1 \times 1 =$

㊳ $7 \times 3 =$

㊴ $8 \times 7 =$

㊵ $9 \times 6 =$

㊶ $6 \times 2 =$

㊷ $7 \times 8 =$

㊸ $1 \times 4 =$

㊹ $8 \times 1 =$

㊺ $9 \times 5 =$

Score

Your Time

min. sec.

/45

38

Practice

Multiplication from 6× to 9×, 1×

Target Time
2 / 3 / 4 min.
* Based on your time from the previous page, circle a target time for completing this page.

Date / / Name

● **Multiply.**

① 7 × 7 =
② 8 × 4 =
③ 6 × 2 =
④ 9 × 6 =
⑤ 1 × 4 =
⑥ 7 × 1 =
⑦ 6 × 8 =
⑧ 8 × 5 =
⑨ 1 × 6 =
⑩ 9 × 4 =
⑪ 7 × 5 =
⑫ 8 × 8 =
⑬ 1 × 1 =
⑭ 6 × 6 =
⑮ 9 × 9 =
⑯ 6 × 4 =
⑰ 7 × 3 =
⑱ 9 × 7 =
⑲ 1 × 5 =
⑳ 6 × 7 =
㉑ 8 × 1 =
㉒ 7 × 8 =
㉓ 9 × 5 =
㉔ 1 × 2 =
㉕ 8 × 6 =
㉖ 9 × 1 =
㉗ 7 × 4 =
㉘ 6 × 9 =
㉙ 8 × 3 =
㉚ 1 × 9 =
㉛ 9 × 3 =
㉜ 7 × 2 =
㉝ 6 × 5 =
㉞ 1 × 8 =
㉟ 8 × 9 =
㊱ 6 × 1 =
㊲ 9 × 8 =
㊳ 7 × 6 =
㊴ 1 × 3 =
㊵ 8 × 7 =
㊶ 9 × 2 =
㊷ 6 × 3 =
㊸ 7 × 9 =
㊹ 1 × 7 =
㊺ 8 × 2 =

Your Time min. sec.

Score /45

39

Practice

Multiplication from 6× to 9×, 1×

Target Time
2 / **3** / **4** min.
* Based on your time from the previous page, circle a target time for completing this page.

Date / / **Name**

● **Multiply.**

① 8 × 6 =
② 9 × 1 =
③ 6 × 5 =
④ 1 × 2 =
⑤ 7 × 9 =
⑥ 8 × 3 =
⑦ 6 × 6 =
⑧ 9 × 4 =
⑨ 7 × 1 =
⑩ 6 × 4 =
⑪ 8 × 8 =
⑫ 1 × 7 =
⑬ 9 × 7 =
⑭ 7 × 2 =
⑮ 1 × 4 =

⑯ 8 × 1 =
⑰ 9 × 5 =
⑱ 1 × 8 =
⑲ 7 × 4 =
⑳ 6 × 1 =
㉑ 1 × 3 =
㉒ 8 × 5 =
㉓ 9 × 2 =
㉔ 6 × 8 =
㉕ 7 × 3 =
㉖ 8 × 9 =
㉗ 1 × 9 =
㉘ 9 × 6 =
㉙ 6 × 2 =
㉚ 7 × 5 =

㉛ 6 × 9 =
㉜ 8 × 4 =
㉝ 1 × 5 =
㉞ 9 × 3 =
㉟ 7 × 6 =
㊱ 6 × 3 =
㊲ 8 × 7 =
㊳ 1 × 6 =
㊴ 9 × 9 =
㊵ 7 × 8 =
㊶ 6 × 7 =
㊷ 8 × 2 =
㊸ 7 × 7 =
㊹ 1 × 1 =
㊺ 9 × 8 =

Your Time min. sec.

Score /45

© Kumon Publishing Co., Ltd.

40

Practice
Multiplication from 6× to 9×, 1×

Target Time

2 / 3 / 4 min.
* Based on your time from the previous page,
circle a target time for completing this page.

| Date | Name |
| / / | |

● **Multiply.**

① 9 × 5 =

② 6 × 8 =

③ 7 × 1 =

④ 1 × 3 =

⑤ 8 × 8 =

⑥ 9 × 7 =

⑦ 6 × 4 =

⑧ 1 × 9 =

⑨ 7 × 4 =

⑩ 8 × 5 =

⑪ 9 × 3 =

⑫ 8 × 9 =

⑬ 1 × 2 =

⑭ 6 × 5 =

⑮ 7 × 7 =

⑯ 9 × 1 =

⑰ 8 × 6 =

⑱ 1 × 8 =

⑲ 6 × 3 =

⑳ 7 × 9 =

㉑ 9 × 4 =

㉒ 1 × 1 =

㉓ 7 × 5 =

㉔ 6 × 7 =

㉕ 8 × 4 =

㉖ 9 × 8 =

㉗ 7 × 3 =

㉘ 8 × 1 =

㉙ 1 × 6 =

㉚ 6 × 2 =

㉛ 9 × 6 =

㉜ 8 × 2 =

㉝ 1 × 7 =

㉞ 6 × 9 =

㉟ 7 × 6 =

㊱ 9 × 2 =

㊲ 6 × 1 =

㊳ 8 × 7 =

㊴ 1 × 4 =

㊵ 7 × 8 =

㊶ 9 × 9 =

㊷ 8 × 3 =

㊸ 1 × 5 =

㊹ 6 × 6 =

㊺ 7 × 2 =

Your Time

min.   sec.

Score

/45

Sprint
Multiplication from 1× to 9×

Date / / Name

● **Multiply. Time how long it takes to complete the multiplication problems. Log your time below.**

① 2 × 5 =

② 5 × 9 =

③ 4 × 8 =

④ 8 × 4 =

⑤ 3 × 1 =

⑥ 7 × 2 =

⑦ 1 × 7 =

⑧ 2 × 2 =

⑨ 6 × 8 =

⑩ 5 × 4 =

⑪ 9 × 2 =

⑫ 3 × 9 =

⑬ 4 × 1 =

⑭ 7 × 7 =

⑮ 6 × 6 =

⑯ 8 × 1 =

⑰ 7 × 9 =

⑱ 3 × 7 =

⑲ 9 × 3 =

⑳ 1 × 8 =

㉑ 5 × 6 =

㉒ 4 × 5 =

㉓ 8 × 7 =

㉔ 6 × 2 =

㉕ 9 × 9 =

㉖ 7 × 5 =

㉗ 2 × 8 =

㉘ 6 × 5 =

㉙ 1 × 4 =

㉚ 3 × 6 =

㉛ 7 × 8 =

㉜ 4 × 3 =

㉝ 9 × 6 =

㉞ 8 × 3 =

㉟ 2 × 9 =

㊱ 1 × 5 =

㊲ 5 × 2 =

㊳ 9 × 8 =

㊴ 3 × 4 =

㊵ 8 × 9 =

㊶ 4 × 7 =

㊷ 6 × 1 =

㊸ 1 × 2 =

㊹ 2 × 6 =

㊺ 5 × 3 =

Review any incorrect answers and remember not to rush.

Score

Your Time

min.   sec.   /45

42

Sprint
Multiplication from 1× to 9×

Target Time
2 / 3 / 4 min.
* Based on your time from the previous page, circle a target time for completing this page.

Date	Name
/ /	

● **Multiply.**

① 3 × 8 =

② 6 × 4 =

③ 8 × 2 =

④ 4 × 9 =

⑤ 1 × 3 =

⑥ 5 × 7 =

⑦ 2 × 3 =

⑧ 9 × 1 =

⑨ 8 × 6 =

⑩ 4 × 2 =

⑪ 3 × 9 =

⑫ 1 × 4 =

⑬ 7 × 8 =

⑭ 6 × 7 =

⑮ 9 × 3 =

⑯ 8 × 3 =

⑰ 5 × 8 =

⑱ 4 × 6 =

⑲ 3 × 3 =

⑳ 6 × 9 =

㉑ 9 × 5 =

㉒ 7 × 1 =

㉓ 8 × 8 =

㉔ 2 × 4 =

㉕ 1 × 6 =

㉖ 6 × 2 =

㉗ 5 × 5 =

㉘ 9 × 4 =

㉙ 4 × 1 =

㉚ 3 × 5 =

㉛ 7 × 3 =

㉜ 4 × 4 =

㉝ 1 × 9 =

㉞ 2 × 7 =

㉟ 8 × 5 =

㊱ 5 × 1 =

㊲ 7 × 6 =

㊳ 3 × 2 =

㊴ 2 × 8 =

㊵ 6 × 3 =

㊶ 7 × 4 =

㊷ 1 × 1 =

㊸ 5 × 2 =

㊹ 9 × 7 =

㊺ 2 × 1 =

Your Time

min.   sec.

Score

/45

Sprint
Multiplication from 1× to 9×

Target Time

2 / 3 / 4 min.

* Based on your time from the previous page, circle a target time for completing this page.

Date   /   /   Name

● **Multiply.**

① 4 × 1 =

② 6 × 3 =

③ 7 × 5 =

④ 8 × 9 =

⑤ 5 × 4 =

⑥ 3 × 1 =

⑦ 9 × 7 =

⑧ 2 × 2 =

⑨ 4 × 4 =

⑩ 6 × 5 =

⑪ 1 × 1 =

⑫ 3 × 9 =

⑬ 5 × 9 =

⑭ 8 × 5 =

⑮ 2 × 6 =

⑯ 9 × 3 =

⑰ 1 × 7 =

⑱ 4 × 6 =

⑲ 6 × 2 =

⑳ 3 × 8 =

㉑ 7 × 3 =

㉒ 5 × 1 =

㉓ 3 × 6 =

㉔ 2 × 9 =

㉕ 8 × 2 =

㉖ 9 × 8 =

㉗ 5 × 5 =

㉘ 4 × 7 =

㉙ 1 × 3 =

㉚ 6 × 8 =

㉛ 7 × 7 =

㉜ 8 × 4 =

㉝ 9 × 2 =

㉞ 6 × 6 =

㉟ 2 × 3 =

㊱ 7 × 4 =

㊲ 9 × 5 =

㊳ 5 × 8 =

㊴ 1 × 6 =

㊵ 4 × 9 =

㊶ 7 × 1 =

㊷ 2 × 5 =

㊸ 3 × 3 =

㊹ 1 × 8 =

㊺ 8 × 7 =

Your Time

min.   sec.

Score

/45

Sprint
Multiplication from 1× to 9×

Target Time

2 / 3 / 4 min.

* Based on your time from the previous page, circle a target time for completing this page.

Date   **Name**

/   /

● **Multiply.**

① 5 × 6 =

② 2 × 8 =

③ 3 × 2 =

④ 9 × 9 =

⑤ 4 × 3 =

⑥ 6 × 7 =

⑦ 8 × 1 =

⑧ 7 × 2 =

⑨ 5 × 8 =

⑩ 1 × 4 =

⑪ 6 × 1 =

⑫ 2 × 9 =

⑬ 3 × 5 =

⑭ 9 × 4 =

⑮ 8 × 7 =

⑯ 4 × 4 =

⑰ 7 × 9 =

⑱ 9 × 5 =

⑲ 5 × 2 =

⑳ 1 × 6 =

㉑ 3 × 7 =

㉒ 6 × 4 =

㉓ 8 × 8 =

㉔ 2 × 1 =

㉕ 4 × 5 =

㉖ 7 × 3 =

㉗ 9 × 6 =

㉘ 1 × 5 =

㉙ 5 × 3 =

㉚ 2 × 7 =

㉛ 7 × 6 =

㉜ 4 × 8 =

㉝ 6 × 2 =

㉞ 3 × 4 =

㉟ 1 × 9 =

㊱ 9 × 1 =

㊲ 8 × 3 =

㊳ 2 × 4 =

㊴ 7 × 8 =

㊵ 1 × 2 =

㊶ 8 × 6 =

㊷ 6 × 9 =

㊸ 4 × 2 =

㊹ 3 × 1 =

㊺ 5 × 7 =

Score

Your Time

min.   sec.   / 45

Sprint
Multiplication from 1× to 9×

Target Time

2 / 3 / 4 min.

* Based on your time from the previous page,
circle a target time for completing this page.

Date / /

Name

● **Multiply.**

① 6 × 9 =

② 7 × 5 =

③ 5 × 2 =

④ 2 × 8 =

⑤ 3 × 1 =

⑥ 8 × 6 =

⑦ 4 × 2 =

⑧ 5 × 4 =

⑨ 7 × 1 =

⑩ 6 × 3 =

⑪ 1 × 4 =

⑫ 2 × 7 =

⑬ 9 × 2 =

⑭ 8 × 1 =

⑮ 3 × 6 =

⑯ 4 × 3 =

⑰ 5 × 7 =

⑱ 7 × 4 =

⑲ 1 × 9 =

⑳ 6 × 6 =

㉑ 2 × 2 =

㉒ 9 × 4 =

㉓ 8 × 7 =

㉔ 4 × 6 =

㉕ 3 × 8 =

㉖ 1 × 2 =

㉗ 5 × 9 =

㉘ 2 × 5 =

㉙ 9 × 6 =

㉚ 7 × 3 =

㉛ 1 × 6 =

㉜ 6 × 1 =

㉝ 4 × 8 =

㉞ 3 × 4 =

㉟ 8 × 3 =

㊱ 9 × 7 =

㊲ 5 × 8 =

㊳ 1 × 1 =

㊴ 7 × 9 =

㊵ 2 × 3 =

㊶ 9 × 8 =

㊷ 4 × 5 =

㊸ 3 × 9 =

㊹ 6 × 7 =

㊺ 8 × 9 =

Score

Your Time

min.   sec.

/45

Sprint
Multiplication from 1× to 9×

Target Time

2 / 3 / 4 min.
* Based on your time from the previous page,
circle a target time for completing this page.

Date   /   /   **Name**

● **Multiply.**

① 8 × 2 =

② 6 × 5 =

③ 2 × 4 =

④ 1 × 7 =

⑤ 9 × 3 =

⑥ 4 × 9 =

⑦ 3 × 7 =

⑧ 7 × 2 =

⑨ 6 × 8 =

⑩ 1 × 3 =

⑪ 5 × 1 =

⑫ 8 × 5 =

⑬ 9 × 8 =

⑭ 6 × 2 =

⑮ 2 × 1 =

⑯ 7 × 6 =

⑰ 5 × 3 =

⑱ 9 × 5 =

⑲ 3 × 2 =

⑳ 4 × 1 =

㉑ 8 × 4 =

㉒ 2 × 6 =

㉓ 3 × 5 =

㉔ 5 × 8 =

㉕ 6 × 9 =

㉖ 7 × 8 =

㉗ 1 × 2 =

㉘ 4 × 4 =

㉙ 3 × 3 =

㉚ 8 × 8 =

㉛ 2 × 7 =

㉜ 1 × 5 =

㉝ 7 × 1 =

㉞ 9 × 9 =

㉟ 5 × 5 =

㊱ 4 × 7 =

㊲ 3 × 6 =

㊳ 8 × 3 =

㊴ 6 × 4 =

㊵ 7 × 7 =

㊶ 4 × 2 =

㊷ 2 × 9 =

㊸ 5 × 6 =

㊹ 1 × 8 =

㊺ 9 × 1 =

Your Time

Score

min.   sec.   /45

Sprint
Multiplication from 1× to 9×

Target Time

2 / 3 / 4 min.

* Based on your time from the previous page, circle a target time for completing this page.

Date / /

Name

● **Multiply.**

① 7 × 3 =

② 5 × 1 =

③ 6 × 2 =

④ 8 × 4 =

⑤ 1 × 9 =

⑥ 9 × 5 =

⑦ 2 × 2 =

⑧ 3 × 6 =

⑨ 4 × 4 =

⑩ 6 × 5 =

⑪ 7 × 7 =

⑫ 1 × 8 =

⑬ 5 × 3 =

⑭ 2 × 5 =

⑮ 4 × 8 =

⑯ 3 × 1 =

⑰ 9 × 3 =

⑱ 6 × 7 =

⑲ 7 × 2 =

⑳ 8 × 9 =

㉑ 5 × 4 =

㉒ 4 × 6 =

㉓ 3 × 4 =

㉔ 2 × 3 =

㉕ 9 × 8 =

㉖ 1 × 6 =

㉗ 6 × 8 =

㉘ 7 × 5 =

㉙ 3 × 9 =

㉚ 8 × 2 =

㉛ 9 × 7 =

㉜ 1 × 4 =

㉝ 2 × 6 =

㉞ 8 × 8 =

㉟ 4 × 1 =

㊱ 5 × 7 =

㊲ 3 × 2 =

㊳ 6 × 3 =

㊴ 7 × 9 =

㊵ 4 × 3 =

㊶ 9 × 4 =

㊷ 2 × 8 =

㊸ 8 × 6 =

㊹ 1 × 1 =

㊺ 5 × 5 =

Your Time

min.   sec.

Score

/45

Sprint
Multiplication from 1× to 9×

Target Time

2 / 3 / 4 min.

* Based on your time from the previous page, circle a target time for completing this page.

Date / /

Name

● **Multiply.**

① 8 × 5 =

② 5 × 2 =

③ 6 × 4 =

④ 3 × 8 =

⑤ 9 × 2 =

⑥ 4 × 5 =

⑦ 2 × 1 =

⑧ 1 × 7 =

⑨ 7 × 4 =

⑩ 5 × 6 =

⑪ 3 × 9 =

⑫ 4 × 3 =

⑬ 8 × 7 =

⑭ 1 × 5 =

⑮ 6 × 1 =

⑯ 9 × 6 =

⑰ 7 × 1 =

⑱ 3 × 7 =

⑲ 2 × 4 =

⑳ 1 × 3 =

㉑ 6 × 9 =

㉒ 5 × 8 =

㉓ 4 × 7 =

㉔ 9 × 1 =

㉕ 8 × 8 =

㉖ 3 × 3 =

㉗ 4 × 9 =

㉘ 7 × 6 =

㉙ 2 × 2 =

㉚ 5 × 9 =

㉛ 1 × 4 =

㉜ 2 × 7 =

㉝ 8 × 3 =

㉞ 4 × 2 =

㉟ 9 × 9 =

㊱ 6 × 5 =

㊲ 7 × 8 =

㊳ 5 × 4 =

㊴ 2 × 9 =

㊵ 3 × 5 =

㊶ 1 × 2 =

㊷ 6 × 6 =

㊸ 8 × 1 =

㊹ 7 × 7 =

㊺ 9 × 3 =

Your Time

min. sec.

Score

/45

Target Time

2 / 3 / 4 min.

* Based on your time from the previous page, circle a target time for completing this page.

Date   /   /

Name

● Multiply.

① $9 \times 8 =$

② $5 \times 1 =$

③ $8 \times 3 =$

④ $4 \times 4 =$

⑤ $3 \times 3 =$

⑥ $7 \times 9 =$

⑦ $6 \times 8 =$

⑧ $1 \times 2 =$

⑨ $4 \times 5 =$

⑩ $2 \times 6 =$

⑪ $7 \times 3 =$

⑫ $9 \times 2 =$

⑬ $8 \times 5 =$

⑭ $3 \times 9 =$

⑮ $5 \times 6 =$

⑯ $1 \times 5 =$

⑰ $2 \times 4 =$

⑱ $7 \times 8 =$

⑲ $8 \times 7 =$

⑳ $9 \times 5 =$

㉑ $4 \times 2 =$

㉒ $3 \times 1 =$

㉓ $1 \times 4 =$

㉔ $5 \times 9 =$

㉕ $6 \times 2 =$

㉖ $7 \times 5 =$

㉗ $4 \times 6 =$

㉘ $1 \times 1 =$

㉙ $2 \times 7 =$

㉚ $6 \times 4 =$

㉛ $5 \times 5 =$

㉜ $8 \times 1 =$

㉝ $9 \times 3 =$

㉞ $3 \times 7 =$

㉟ $1 \times 9 =$

㊱ $6 \times 6 =$

㊲ $7 \times 1 =$

㊳ $2 \times 2 =$

㊴ $4 \times 7 =$

㊵ $8 \times 8 =$

㊶ $5 \times 3 =$

㊷ $3 \times 5 =$

㊸ $6 \times 1 =$

㊹ $9 \times 9 =$

㊺ $2 \times 8 =$

Your Time

min.   sec.

Score

/45

Sprint
Multiplication from 1× to 9×

Target Time

2 / **3** / **4** min.

* Based on your time from the previous page, circle a target time for completing this page.

Date

/   /

Name

● **Multiply.**

① 1 × 6 =

② 4 × 3 =

③ 3 × 8 =

④ 5 × 2 =

⑤ 6 × 4 =

⑥ 2 × 1 =

⑦ 7 × 7 =

⑧ 4 × 5 =

⑨ 3 × 2 =

⑩ 8 × 4 =

⑪ 9 × 7 =

⑫ 5 × 8 =

⑬ 1 × 4 =

⑭ 6 × 9 =

⑮ 2 × 6 =

⑯ 4 × 9 =

⑰ 8 × 6 =

⑱ 5 × 4 =

⑲ 3 × 7 =

⑳ 2 × 3 =

㉑ 7 × 2 =

㉒ 9 × 1 =

㉓ 1 × 8 =

㉔ 6 × 7 =

㉕ 3 × 4 =

㉖ 8 × 1 =

㉗ 7 × 6 =

㉘ 2 × 5 =

㉙ 4 × 8 =

㉚ 5 × 3 =

㉛ 9 × 6 =

㉜ 6 × 3 =

㉝ 1 × 7 =

㉞ 8 × 9 =

㉟ 7 × 5 =

㊱ 3 × 6 =

㊲ 9 × 4 =

㊳ 8 × 2 =

㊴ 4 × 1 =

㊵ 9 × 8 =

㊶ 7 × 4 =

㊷ 2 × 9 =

㊸ 5 × 7 =

㊹ 1 × 3 =

㊺ 6 × 5 =

Your Time

min.   sec.

Score

/45

Target Time

2 / 3 / 4 min.

Based on your time from the previous page, circle a target time for completing this page.

Date / /

Name

● **Multiply.**

① 2 × 2 =

② 1 × 8 =

③ 6 × 5 =

④ 7 × 6 =

⑤ 9 × 4 =

⑥ 8 × 3 =

⑦ 4 × 1 =

⑧ 6 × 7 =

⑨ 1 × 5 =

⑩ 5 × 6 =

⑪ 9 × 8 =

⑫ 7 × 4 =

⑬ 3 × 1 =

⑭ 2 × 9 =

⑮ 4 × 3 =

⑯ 5 × 1 =

⑰ 1 × 7 =

⑱ 3 × 3 =

⑲ 4 × 8 =

⑳ 1 × 2 =

㉑ 7 × 9 =

㉒ 8 × 5 =

㉓ 9 × 6 =

㉔ 5 × 4 =

㉕ 2 × 7 =

㉖ 6 × 1 =

㉗ 8 × 9 =

㉘ 4 × 5 =

㉙ 3 × 6 =

㉚ 7 × 2 =

㉛ 2 × 5 =

㉜ 8 × 2 =

㉝ 9 × 7 =

㉞ 3 × 8 =

㉟ 4 × 4 =

㊱ 6 × 8 =

㊲ 5 × 3 =

㊳ 9 × 2 =

㊴ 3 × 9 =

㊵ 7 × 1 =

㊶ 6 × 3 =

㊷ 2 × 4 =

㊸ 8 × 7 =

㊹ 5 × 8 =

㊺ 1 × 3 =

Your Time

min.   sec.

Score

/45

Sprint
Multiplication from 1× to 9×

Target Time
2 / 3 / 4 min.
Based on your time from the previous page, circle a target time for completing this page.

Date / /   **Name**

● **Multiply.**

① 3 × 5 =

② 2 × 8 =

③ 9 × 4 =

④ 1 × 9 =

⑤ 7 × 3 =

⑥ 8 × 8 =

⑦ 4 × 2 =

⑧ 6 × 6 =

⑨ 2 × 1 =

⑩ 5 × 2 =

⑪ 9 × 5 =

⑫ 4 × 4 =

⑬ 3 × 2 =

⑭ 7 × 8 =

⑮ 1 × 4 =

⑯ 4 × 9 =

⑰ 8 × 1 =

⑱ 9 × 3 =

⑲ 6 × 7 =

⑳ 1 × 2 =

㉑ 3 × 4 =

㉒ 2 × 3 =

㉓ 7 × 6 =

㉔ 5 × 9 =

㉕ 4 × 7 =

㉖ 8 × 6 =

㉗ 1 × 1 =

㉘ 9 × 9 =

㉙ 5 × 5 =

㉚ 6 × 2 =

㉛ 8 × 4 =

㉜ 3 × 1 =

㉝ 5 × 3 =

㉞ 7 × 7 =

㉟ 1 × 6 =

㊱ 6 × 4 =

㊲ 2 × 5 =

㊳ 8 × 3 =

㊴ 4 × 6 =

㊵ 5 × 7 =

㊶ 9 × 1 =

㊷ 3 × 7 =

㊸ 2 × 6 =

㊹ 6 × 9 =

㊺ 7 × 5 =

Your Time
min.   sec.

Score
/45

Sprint
Multiplication from 1× to 9×

Target Time

2 / 3 / 4 min.

* Based on your time from the previous page, circle a target time for completing this page.

Date

/   /

Name

● **Multiply.**

① 4 × 8 =

② 8 × 9 =

③ 1 × 4 =

④ 5 × 8 =

⑤ 7 × 6 =

⑥ 2 × 1 =

⑦ 4 × 3 =

⑧ 3 × 5 =

⑨ 8 × 6 =

⑩ 1 × 2 =

⑪ 5 × 7 =

⑫ 7 × 8 =

⑬ 9 × 3 =

⑭ 2 × 9 =

⑮ 6 × 6 =

⑯ 5 × 2 =

⑰ 4 × 5 =

⑱ 9 × 9 =

⑲ 8 × 3 =

⑳ 3 × 2 =

㉑ 1 × 7 =

㉒ 7 × 4 =

㉓ 2 × 6 =

㉔ 5 × 5 =

㉕ 6 × 8 =

㉖ 4 × 1 =

㉗ 9 × 4 =

㉘ 3 × 7 =

㉙ 1 × 9 =

㉚ 6 × 3 =

㉛ 2 × 4 =

㉜ 9 × 6 =

㉝ 3 × 1 =

㉞ 7 × 2 =

㉟ 6 × 9 =

㊱ 8 × 7 =

㊲ 5 × 3 =

㊳ 6 × 1 =

㊴ 4 × 7 =

㊵ 9 × 2 =

㊶ 2 × 8 =

㊷ 1 × 5 =

㊸ 8 × 1 =

㊹ 3 × 4 =

㊺ 7 × 9 =

Score

Your Time

min.   sec.

/45

54 Sprint Multiplication from 1× to 9×

Target Time

2 / 3 / 4 min.

* Based on your time from the previous page, circle a target time for completing this page.

Date / /

Name

● **Multiply.**

① 5 × 4 =

② 4 × 9 =

③ 2 × 2 =

④ 7 × 1 =

⑤ 1 × 8 =

⑥ 6 × 2 =

⑦ 8 × 7 =

⑧ 5 × 1 =

⑨ 9 × 5 =

⑩ 3 × 3 =

⑪ 7 × 7 =

⑫ 2 × 3 =

⑬ 4 × 2 =

⑭ 1 × 9 =

⑮ 6 × 4 =

⑯ 3 × 8 =

⑰ 8 × 4 =

⑱ 5 × 6 =

⑲ 4 × 5 =

⑳ 2 × 7 =

㉑ 1 × 3 =

㉒ 9 × 7 =

㉓ 6 × 5 =

㉔ 7 × 4 =

㉕ 3 × 9 =

㉖ 9 × 2 =

㉗ 8 × 5 =

㉘ 4 × 6 =

㉙ 2 × 8 =

㉚ 5 × 9 =

㉛ 1 × 6 =

㉜ 3 × 2 =

㉝ 9 × 1 =

㉞ 6 × 7 =

㉟ 7 × 3 =

㊱ 8 × 8 =

㊲ 5 × 3 =

㊳ 7 × 5 =

㊴ 4 × 4 =

㊵ 9 × 8 =

㊶ 3 × 6 =

㊷ 1 × 1 =

㊸ 6 × 9 =

㊹ 2 × 5 =

㊺ 8 × 2 =

Your Time min. sec.

Score /45

55

Sprint
Multiplication from 1× to 9×

Target Time

2 / 3 / 4 min.

* Based on your time from the previous page, circle a target time for completing this page.

Date   /   /

Name

● **Multiply.**

① 6 × 1 =

② 1 × 2 =

③ 5 × 7 =

④ 9 × 5 =

⑤ 2 × 3 =

⑥ 8 × 4 =

⑦ 3 × 2 =

⑧ 7 × 6 =

⑨ 4 × 3 =

⑩ 1 × 9 =

⑪ 9 × 4 =

⑫ 6 × 3 =

⑬ 8 × 6 =

⑭ 5 × 9 =

⑮ 2 × 1 =

⑯ 7 × 7 =

⑰ 3 × 1 =

⑱ 4 × 9 =

⑲ 5 × 2 =

⑳ 8 × 8 =

㉑ 7 × 2 =

㉒ 6 × 6 =

㉓ 4 × 4 =

㉔ 9 × 7 =

㉕ 1 × 3 =

㉖ 3 × 8 =

㉗ 8 × 2 =

㉘ 5 × 5 =

㉙ 2 × 8 =

㉚ 7 × 1 =

㉛ 3 × 6 =

㉜ 7 × 3 =

㉝ 6 × 5 =

㉞ 2 × 4 =

㉟ 4 × 6 =

㊱ 9 × 9 =

㊲ 1 × 8 =

㊳ 5 × 3 =

㊴ 8 × 5 =

㊵ 9 × 2 =

㊶ 1 × 7 =

㊷ 6 × 8 =

㊸ 4 × 1 =

㊹ 3 × 4 =

㊺ 2 × 5 =

Score

Your Time

min.   sec.

/45

Sprint
Multiplication from 1× to 9×

Target Time

2 / 3 / 4 min.

* Based on your time from the previous page,
circle a target time for completing this page.

Date / /   **Name**

● **Multiply.**

① 7 × 9 =

② 1 × 4 =

③ 6 × 2 =

④ 2 × 7 =

⑤ 3 × 9 =

⑥ 9 × 1 =

⑦ 8 × 3 =

⑧ 4 × 8 =

⑨ 6 × 7 =

⑩ 3 × 5 =

⑪ 5 × 6 =

⑫ 7 × 4 =

⑬ 2 × 2 =

⑭ 1 × 5 =

⑮ 9 × 3 =

⑯ 2 × 3 =

⑰ 8 × 9 =

⑱ 5 × 7 =

⑲ 4 × 2 =

⑳ 7 × 5 =

㉑ 3 × 1 =

㉒ 6 × 6 =

㉓ 4 × 7 =

㉔ 9 × 8 =

㉕ 1 × 6 =

㉖ 5 × 4 =

㉗ 2 × 9 =

㉘ 3 × 3 =

㉙ 8 × 1 =

㉚ 7 × 8 =

㉛ 1 × 2 =

㉜ 8 × 4 =

㉝ 5 × 1 =

㉞ 9 × 7 =

㉟ 4 × 5 =

㊱ 6 × 4 =

㊲ 2 × 6 =

㊳ 3 × 7 =

㊴ 7 × 3 =

㊵ 4 × 9 =

㊶ 9 × 6 =

㊷ 1 × 1 =

㊸ 5 × 8 =

㊹ 8 × 7 =

㊺ 6 × 9 =

Congratulations!
You have really
improved your
speed and accuracy!

Your Time

min.   sec.

Score

/45

Answer Key
Multiplication

---

1 — Warm-Up: Multiplication 2×

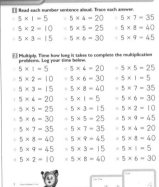

1 Read each number sentence aloud. Trace each answer.

2×1=2	2×4=8	2×7=14
2×2=4	2×5=10	2×8=16
2×3=6	2×6=12	2×9=18

2 Multiply. Time how long it takes to complete the multiplication problems. Log your time below.

2×1=2	2×3=6	2×9=18
2×2=4	2×5=10	2×4=8
2×3=6	2×7=14	2×2=4
2×4=8	2×9=18	2×2=4
2×5=10	2×2=4	2×6=12
2×6=12	2×4=8	2×3=6
2×7=14	2×6=12	2×8=16
2×8=16	2×8=16	2×4=8
2×9=18	2×1=2	2×2=4
2×1=2	2×5=10	2×5=10

Review any incorrect answers and remember not to rush.

---

2 — Warm-Up: Multiplication 3×

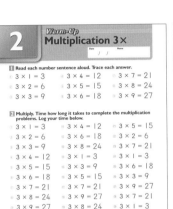

1 Read each number sentence aloud. Trace each answer.

3×1=3	3×4=12	3×7=21
3×2=6	3×5=15	3×8=24
3×3=9	3×6=18	3×9=27

2 Multiply. Time how long it takes to complete the multiplication problems. Log your time below.

3×1=3	3×4=12	3×5=15
3×2=6	3×6=18	3×2=6
3×3=9	3×8=24	3×7=21
3×4=12	3×1=3	3×1=3
3×5=15	3×3=9	3×6=18
3×6=18	3×2=6	3×3=9
3×7=21	3×7=21	3×9=27
3×8=24	3×9=27	3×7=21
3×9=27	3×8=24	3×1=3
3×2=6	3×4=12	3×8=24

---

3 — Warm-Up: Multiplication 4×

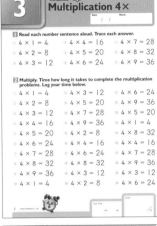

1 Read each number sentence aloud. Trace each answer.

4×1=4	4×4=16	4×7=28
4×2=8	4×5=20	4×8=32
4×3=12	4×6=24	4×9=36

2 Multiply. Time how long it takes to complete the multiplication problems. Log your time below.

4×1=4	4×3=12	4×6=24
4×2=8	4×5=20	4×9=36
4×3=12	4×7=28	4×5=20
4×4=16	4×9=36	4×1=4
4×5=20	4×2=8	4×8=32
4×6=24	4×4=16	4×4=16
4×7=28	4×6=24	4×7=28
4×8=32	4×8=32	4×9=36
4×9=36	4×3=12	4×3=12
4×1=4	4×2=8	4×2=8

---

4 — Warm-Up: Review: Multiplication from 2× to 4×

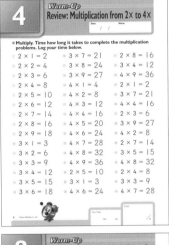

Multiply. Time how long it takes to complete the multiplication problems. Log your time below.

2×1=2	3×7=21	2×8=16
2×2=4	3×8=24	3×4=12
2×3=6	3×9=27	4×9=36
2×4=8	4×1=4	2×1=2
2×5=10	4×2=8	3×7=21
2×6=12	4×3=12	4×4=16
2×7=14	4×4=16	2×3=6
2×8=16	4×5=20	3×9=27
2×9=18	4×6=24	4×2=8
3×1=3	4×7=28	2×7=14
3×2=6	4×8=32	3×5=15
3×3=9	4×9=36	4×8=32
3×4=12	2×5=10	2×4=8
3×5=15	3×1=3	3×3=9
3×6=18	4×6=24	2×7=14

---

5 — Warm-Up: Multiplication 5×

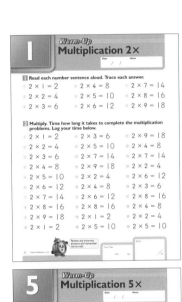

1 Read each number sentence aloud. Trace each answer.

5×1=5	5×4=20	5×7=35
5×2=10	5×5=25	5×8=40
5×3=15	5×6=30	5×9=45

2 Multiply. Time how long it takes to complete the multiplication problems. Log your time below.

5×1=5	5×4=20	5×5=25
5×2=10	5×6=30	5×1=5
5×3=15	5×8=40	5×7=35
5×4=20	5×1=5	5×6=30
5×5=25	5×3=15	5×2=10
5×6=30	5×5=25	5×9=45
5×7=35	5×7=35	5×4=20
5×8=40	5×9=45	5×8=40
5×9=45	5×3=15	5×1=5
5×2=10	5×8=40	5×6=30

---

6 — Warm-Up: Multiplication 6×

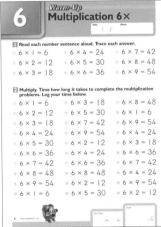

1 Read each number sentence aloud. Trace each answer.

6×1=6	6×4=24	6×7=42
6×2=12	6×5=30	6×8=48
6×3=18	6×6=36	6×9=54

2 Multiply. Time how long it takes to complete the multiplication problems. Log your time below.

6×1=6	6×3=18	6×8=48
6×2=12	6×5=30	6×1=6
6×3=18	6×7=42	6×9=54
6×4=24	6×9=54	6×4=24
6×5=30	6×2=12	6×3=18
6×6=36	6×4=24	6×6=36
6×7=42	6×6=36	6×7=42
6×8=48	6×8=48	6×4=24
6×9=54	6×2=12	6×9=54
6×5=30	6×5=30	6×2=12

---

7 — Warm-Up: Multiplication 7×

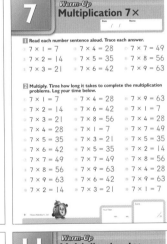

1 Read each number sentence aloud. Trace each answer.

7×1=7	7×4=28	7×7=49
7×2=14	7×5=35	7×8=56
7×3=21	7×6=42	7×9=63

2 Multiply. Time how long it takes to complete the multiplication problems. Log your time below.

7×1=7	7×4=28	7×9=63
7×2=14	7×6=42	7×1=7
7×3=21	7×8=56	7×4=28
7×4=28	7×1=7	7×7=49
7×5=35	7×3=21	7×5=35
7×6=42	7×5=35	7×2=14
7×7=49	7×7=49	7×8=56
7×8=56	7×9=63	7×4=28
7×9=63	7×6=42	7×9=63
7×2=14	7×3=21	7×1=7

---

8 — Warm-Up: Review: Multiplication from 5× to 7×

Multiply. Time how long it takes to complete the multiplication problems. Log your time below.

5×1=5	6×7=42	5×5=25
5×2=10	6×8=48	6×4=24
5×3=15	6×9=54	7×9=63
5×4=20	7×1=7	5×6=30
5×5=25	7×2=14	6×1=6
5×6=30	7×3=21	7×4=28
5×7=35	7×4=28	5×9=45
5×8=40	7×5=35	6×2=12
5×9=45	7×6=42	7×6=42
6×1=6	7×7=49	5×1=5
6×2=12	7×8=56	6×7=42
6×3=18	7×9=63	7×2=14
6×4=24	5×2=10	5×8=40
6×5=30	6×8=48	6×5=30
6×6=36	7×3=21	7×7=49

---

9 — Warm-Up: Multiplication 8×

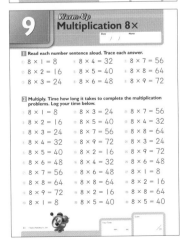

1 Read each number sentence aloud. Trace each answer.

8×1=8	8×4=32	8×7=56
8×2=16	8×5=40	8×8=64
8×3=24	8×6=48	8×9=72

2 Multiply. Time how long it takes to complete the multiplication problems. Log your time below.

8×1=8	8×3=24	8×7=56
8×2=16	8×5=40	8×4=32
8×3=24	8×7=56	8×8=64
8×4=32	8×9=72	8×3=24
8×5=40	8×2=16	8×9=72
8×6=48	8×4=32	8×6=48
8×7=56	8×6=48	8×1=8
8×8=64	8×8=64	8×2=16
8×9=72	8×2=16	8×8=64
8×1=8	8×5=40	8×5=40

---

10 — Warm-Up: Multiplication 9×

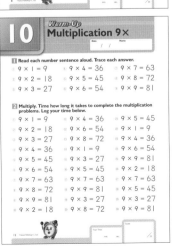

1 Read each number sentence aloud. Trace each answer.

9×1=9	9×4=36	9×7=63
9×2=18	9×5=45	9×8=72
9×3=27	9×6=54	9×9=81

2 Multiply. Time how long it takes to complete the multiplication problems. Log your time below.

9×1=9	9×4=36	9×5=45
9×2=18	9×6=54	9×1=9
9×3=27	9×8=72	9×4=36
9×4=36	9×1=9	9×6=54
9×5=45	9×3=27	9×9=81
9×6=54	9×5=45	9×2=18
9×7=63	9×7=63	9×7=63
9×8=72	9×9=81	9×3=27
9×9=81	9×3=27	9×3=27
9×2=18	9×8=72	9×9=81

---

11 — Warm-Up: Multiplication 1×

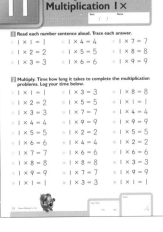

1 Read each number sentence aloud. Trace each answer.

1×1=1	1×4=4	1×7=7
1×2=2	1×5=5	1×8=8
1×3=3	1×6=6	1×9=9

2 Multiply. Time how long it takes to complete the multiplication problems. Log your time below.

1×1=1	1×3=3	1×8=8
1×2=2	1×5=5	1×1=1
1×3=3	1×7=7	1×4=4
1×4=4	1×9=9	1×9=9
1×5=5	1×2=2	1×5=5
1×6=6	1×4=4	1×2=2
1×7=7	1×6=6	1×6=6
1×8=8	1×8=8	1×3=3
1×9=9	1×2=2	1×9=9
1×1=1	1×3=3	1×1=1

---

12 — Warm-Up: Review: Multiplication 8×, 9×, 1×

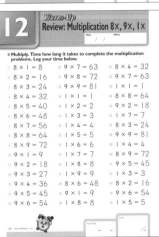

Multiply. Time how long it takes to complete the multiplication problems. Log your time below.

8×1=8	9×7=63	8×4=32
8×2=16	9×8=72	9×7=63
8×3=24	9×9=81	1×1=1
8×4=32	1×1=1	8×8=64
8×5=40	1×2=2	9×2=18
8×6=48	1×3=3	1×7=7
8×7=56	1×4=4	8×3=24
8×8=64	1×5=5	9×9=81
8×9=72	1×6=6	1×4=4
9×1=9	1×7=7	8×9=72
9×2=18	1×8=8	9×5=45
9×3=27	8×9=72	1×3=3
9×4=36	8×6=48	8×2=16
9×5=45	9×1=9	9×2=54
9×6=54	1×8=8	1×5=5

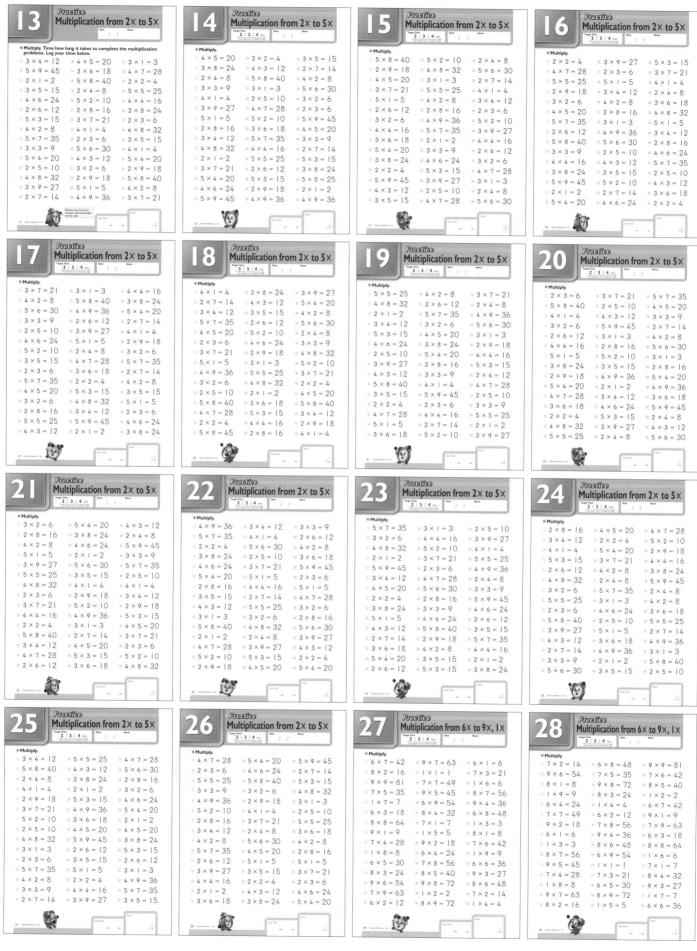

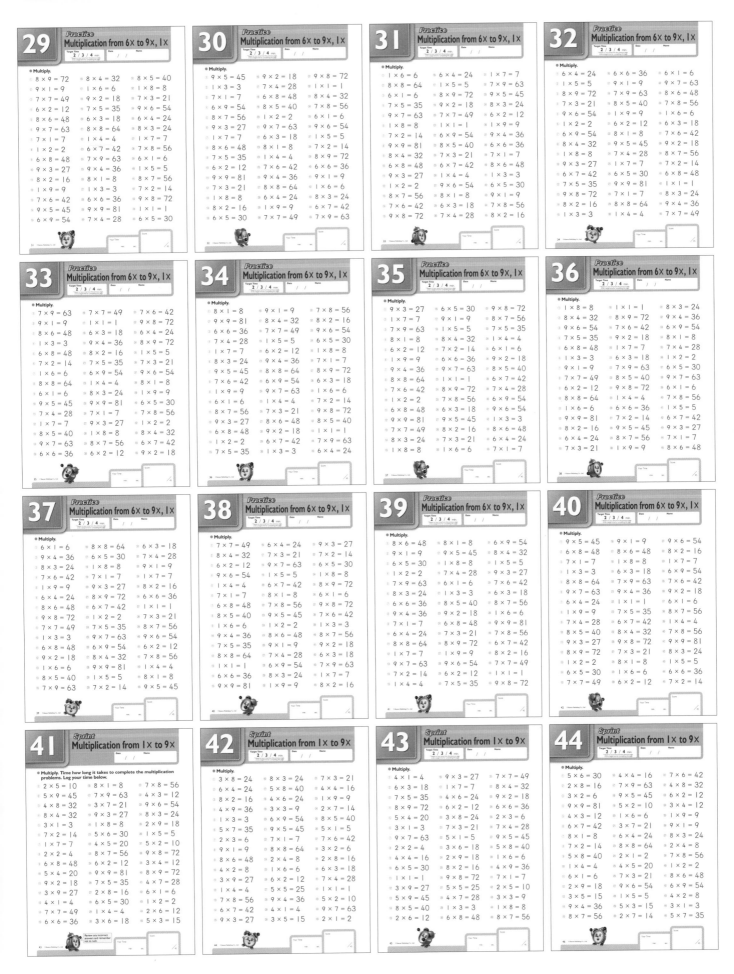

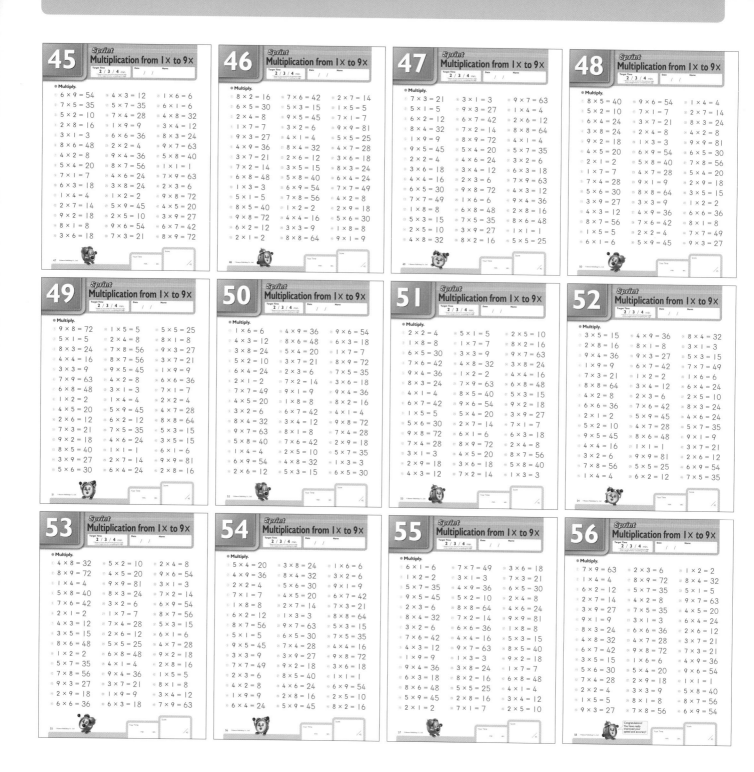

45 — Sprint: Multiplication from 1× to 9×
Target Time 2 / 3 / 4 min. · Date / / · Name

● Multiply.

6 × 9 = 54	4 × 3 = 12	1 × 6 = 6
7 × 5 = 35	5 × 7 = 35	6 × 1 = 6
5 × 2 = 10	7 × 4 = 28	4 × 8 = 32
2 × 8 = 16	1 × 9 = 9	3 × 4 = 12
3 × 1 = 3	6 × 6 = 36	8 × 3 = 24
8 × 6 = 48	2 × 2 = 4	9 × 7 = 63
4 × 2 = 8	9 × 4 = 36	5 × 8 = 40
5 × 4 = 20	8 × 7 = 56	1 × 1 = 1
7 × 1 = 7	4 × 6 = 24	7 × 9 = 63
6 × 3 = 18	3 × 8 = 24	2 × 3 = 6
1 × 4 = 4	5 × 1 = 5	8 × 9 = 72
2 × 7 = 14	5 × 9 = 45	4 × 5 = 20
9 × 2 = 18	2 × 5 = 10	3 × 9 = 27
8 × 1 = 8	9 × 6 = 54	6 × 7 = 42
3 × 6 = 18	7 × 3 = 21	8 × 9 = 72

46 — Sprint: Multiplication from 1× to 9×
Target Time 2 / 3 / 4 min. · Date / / · Name

● Multiply.

8 × 2 = 16	7 × 6 = 42	2 × 7 = 14
6 × 5 = 30	5 × 3 = 15	1 × 5 = 5
2 × 4 = 8	9 × 5 = 45	7 × 1 = 7
1 × 7 = 7	3 × 2 = 6	9 × 9 = 81
9 × 3 = 27	4 × 1 = 4	5 × 5 = 25
4 × 9 = 36	8 × 4 = 32	4 × 7 = 28
3 × 7 = 21	2 × 6 = 12	3 × 6 = 18
7 × 2 = 14	3 × 5 = 15	4 × 3 = 12
6 × 8 = 48	5 × 8 = 40	6 × 4 = 24
1 × 3 = 3	6 × 9 = 54	7 × 7 = 49
5 × 1 = 5	7 × 8 = 56	4 × 2 = 8
8 × 5 = 40	1 × 2 = 2	2 × 9 = 18
9 × 8 = 72	4 × 4 = 16	5 × 6 = 30
6 × 2 = 12	3 × 3 = 9	1 × 8 = 8
	8 × 8 = 64	9 × 1 = 9

47 — Sprint: Multiplication from 1× to 9×
Target Time 2 / 3 / 4 min. · Date / / · Name

● Multiply.

7 × 3 = 21	3 × 1 = 3	9 × 7 = 63
5 × 1 = 5	9 × 3 = 27	1 × 4 = 4
6 × 2 = 12	6 × 7 = 42	2 × 6 = 12
8 × 4 = 32	7 × 2 = 14	8 × 8 = 64
1 × 9 = 9	8 × 9 = 72	4 × 1 = 4
9 × 5 = 45	5 × 4 = 20	5 × 7 = 35
2 × 2 = 4	4 × 6 = 24	3 × 2 = 6
1 × 8 = 8	3 × 4 = 12	6 × 3 = 18
4 × 4 = 16	2 × 3 = 6	7 × 9 = 63
6 × 5 = 30	9 × 8 = 72	4 × 3 = 12
7 × 7 = 49	1 × 6 = 6	9 × 4 = 36
1 × 8 = 8	6 × 8 = 48	2 × 8 = 16
5 × 3 = 15	7 × 5 = 35	8 × 6 = 48
2 × 5 = 10	3 × 9 = 27	1 × 1 = 1
4 × 8 = 32	8 × 2 = 16	5 × 5 = 25

48 — Sprint: Multiplication from 1× to 9×
Target Time 2 / 3 / 4 min. · Date / / · Name

● Multiply.

8 × 5 = 40	9 × 6 = 54	1 × 4 = 4
5 × 2 = 10	1 × 7 = 7	2 × 7 = 14
6 × 4 = 24	3 × 7 = 21	8 × 3 = 24
3 × 8 = 24	2 × 4 = 8	4 × 2 = 8
9 × 2 = 18	1 × 3 = 3	9 × 9 = 81
4 × 9 = 36	6 × 9 = 54	6 × 5 = 30
2 × 1 = 2	5 × 8 = 40	7 × 8 = 56
1 × 7 = 7	4 × 7 = 28	5 × 4 = 20
4 × 7 = 28	9 × 1 = 9	2 × 9 = 18
5 × 6 = 30	8 × 4 = 64	3 × 5 = 15
3 × 9 = 27	3 × 3 = 9	1 × 2 = 2
4 × 3 = 12	4 × 9 = 36	6 × 6 = 36
5 × 7 = 56	7 × 6 = 42	4 × 7 = 49
1 × 5 = 5	8 × 1 = 8	7 × 7 = 49
6 × 1 = 6	5 × 9 = 45	9 × 3 = 27

49 — Sprint: Multiplication from 1× to 9×
Target Time 2 / 3 / 4 min. · Date / / · Name

● Multiply.

9 × 8 = 72	1 × 5 = 5	5 × 5 = 25
5 × 1 = 5	2 × 4 = 8	8 × 1 = 8
8 × 3 = 24	1 × 7 = 7	9 × 3 = 27
4 × 4 = 16	8 × 7 = 56	3 × 7 = 21
3 × 3 = 9	9 × 5 = 45	1 × 9 = 9
7 × 9 = 63	4 × 2 = 8	6 × 6 = 36
6 × 8 = 48	3 × 1 = 3	7 × 1 = 7
1 × 2 = 2	1 × 4 = 4	2 × 2 = 4
4 × 5 = 20	5 × 9 = 45	4 × 7 = 28
2 × 6 = 12	6 × 2 = 12	8 × 8 = 64
7 × 3 = 21	7 × 5 = 35	5 × 3 = 15
9 × 2 = 18	4 × 6 = 24	3 × 5 = 15
8 × 5 = 40	1 × 1 = 1	6 × 1 = 6
3 × 9 = 27	6 × 6 = 36	9 × 9 = 81
5 × 6 = 30	6 × 4 = 24	9 × 8 = 16

50 — Sprint: Multiplication from 1× to 9×
Target Time 2 / 3 / 4 min. · Date / / · Name

● Multiply.

1 × 6 = 6	4 × 9 = 36	9 × 6 = 54
4 × 3 = 12	8 × 6 = 48	6 × 3 = 18
3 × 8 = 24	5 × 4 = 20	1 × 7 = 7
5 × 2 = 10	3 × 7 = 21	4 × 9 = 72
6 × 4 = 24	2 × 3 = 6	7 × 5 = 35
2 × 1 = 2	7 × 2 = 14	3 × 6 = 18
7 × 7 = 49	9 × 1 = 9	9 × 4 = 36
4 × 5 = 20	1 × 8 = 8	8 × 2 = 16
3 × 2 = 6	6 × 7 = 42	4 × 1 = 4
8 × 4 = 32	3 × 4 = 12	9 × 8 = 72
9 × 7 = 63	8 × 1 = 8	7 × 4 = 28
5 × 8 = 40	7 × 6 = 42	2 × 9 = 18
1 × 4 = 4	2 × 5 = 10	5 × 7 = 35
6 × 9 = 54	4 × 8 = 32	1 × 3 = 3
2 × 6 = 12	5 × 3 = 15	6 × 5 = 30

51 — Sprint: Multiplication from 1× to 9×
Target Time 2 / 3 / 4 min. · Date / / · Name

● Multiply.

2 × 2 = 4	5 × 1 = 5	2 × 5 = 10
1 × 8 = 8	1 × 7 = 7	8 × 2 = 16
6 × 5 = 30	3 × 3 = 9	9 × 7 = 63
7 × 6 = 42	4 × 8 = 32	3 × 8 = 24
9 × 4 = 36	1 × 2 = 2	4 × 4 = 16
8 × 3 = 24	7 × 9 = 63	6 × 8 = 48
1 × 4 = 4	8 × 5 = 40	5 × 3 = 15
6 × 7 = 42	5 × 9 = 54	9 × 2 = 18
1 × 5 = 5	5 × 4 = 20	3 × 9 = 27
5 × 6 = 30	2 × 7 = 14	7 × 1 = 7
9 × 8 = 72	6 × 9 = 72	6 × 3 = 18
7 × 4 = 28	8 × 9 = 72	2 × 4 = 8
3 × 1 = 3	4 × 5 = 20	8 × 7 = 56
2 × 9 = 18	3 × 6 = 18	5 × 8 = 40
4 × 3 = 12	7 × 2 = 14	1 × 3 = 3

52 — Sprint: Multiplication from 1× to 9×
Target Time 2 / 3 / 4 min. · Date / / · Name

● Multiply.

3 × 5 = 15	4 × 9 = 36	8 × 4 = 32
2 × 8 = 16	8 × 1 = 8	3 × 1 = 3
9 × 4 = 36	9 × 3 = 27	5 × 3 = 15
1 × 9 = 9	6 × 7 = 42	7 × 7 = 49
7 × 3 = 21	1 × 2 = 2	1 × 6 = 6
8 × 8 = 64	3 × 4 = 12	6 × 4 = 24
4 × 2 = 8	2 × 3 = 6	2 × 5 = 10
6 × 3 = 36	7 × 6 = 42	8 × 3 = 24
2 × 1 = 2	5 × 9 = 45	4 × 6 = 24
5 × 2 = 10	4 × 7 = 28	5 × 7 = 35
9 × 5 = 45	8 × 6 = 48	9 × 1 = 9
3 × 2 = 6	1 × 1 = 1	3 × 7 = 21
7 × 8 = 56	5 × 5 = 25	6 × 9 = 54
1 × 4 = 4	6 × 2 = 12	7 × 5 = 35

53 — Sprint: Multiplication from 1× to 9×
Target Time 2 / 3 / 4 min. · Date / / · Name

● Multiply.

4 × 8 = 32	5 × 2 = 10	2 × 4 = 8
8 × 4 = 20	4 × 5 = 20	9 × 6 = 54
1 × 4 = 4	9 × 9 = 81	3 × 1 = 3
5 × 8 = 40	8 × 3 = 24	7 × 2 = 14
6 × 7 = 42	4 × 2 = 6	6 × 9 = 54
2 × 1 = 2	1 × 7 = 7	8 × 7 = 56
4 × 3 = 12	7 × 4 = 28	5 × 3 = 15
3 × 5 = 15	2 × 6 = 12	6 × 1 = 6
6 × 8 = 48	5 × 5 = 25	4 × 7 = 28
1 × 2 = 2	6 × 8 = 48	9 × 2 = 18
5 × 7 = 35	4 × 1 = 4	2 × 8 = 16
7 × 8 = 56	9 × 4 = 36	1 × 5 = 5
3 × 7 = 21	3 × 7 = 21	8 × 1 = 8
2 × 9 = 18	1 × 9 = 9	3 × 4 = 12
6 × 6 = 36	6 × 3 = 18	7 × 9 = 63

54 — Sprint: Multiplication from 1× to 9×
Target Time 2 / 3 / 4 min. · Date / / · Name

● Multiply.

5 × 4 = 20	3 × 8 = 24	1 × 6 = 6
4 × 9 = 36	8 × 4 = 32	3 × 2 = 6
2 × 2 = 4	5 × 9 = 30	9 × 1 = 9
7 × 1 = 7	4 × 5 = 20	6 × 7 = 42
1 × 8 = 8	2 × 7 = 14	7 × 3 = 21
6 × 2 = 12	1 × 3 = 3	8 × 8 = 64
8 × 7 = 56	9 × 7 = 63	5 × 3 = 15
5 × 1 = 5	6 × 5 = 30	7 × 5 = 35
9 × 5 = 45	7 × 4 = 28	4 × 4 = 16
3 × 3 = 9	9 × 2 = 18	9 × 8 = 72
7 × 7 = 49	8 × 5 = 40	3 × 6 = 18
2 × 3 = 6	8 × 5 = 40	1 × 1 = 1
4 × 2 = 8	4 × 6 = 24	9 × 4 = 54
8 × 3 = 24	2 × 8 = 16	2 × 5 = 10
6 × 4 = 24	5 × 9 = 45	8 × 2 = 16

55 — Sprint: Multiplication from 1× to 9×
Target Time 2 / 3 / 4 min. · Date / / · Name

● Multiply.

6 × 1 = 6	7 × 7 = 49	3 × 6 = 18
1 × 2 = 2	3 × 1 = 3	7 × 3 = 21
3 × 5 = 15	4 × 9 = 36	6 × 5 = 30
9 × 5 = 45	5 × 2 = 10	2 × 4 = 8
2 × 3 = 6	8 × 8 = 64	4 × 6 = 24
8 × 4 = 32	7 × 2 = 14	9 × 9 = 81
3 × 2 = 6	6 × 6 = 36	1 × 8 = 8
7 × 6 = 42	4 × 4 = 16	5 × 3 = 15
4 × 3 = 12	9 × 7 = 63	8 × 5 = 40
1 × 9 = 9	1 × 3 = 3	9 × 2 = 18
9 × 4 = 36	3 × 8 = 24	1 × 7 = 7
6 × 3 = 18	8 × 2 = 16	6 × 8 = 48
8 × 6 = 48	5 × 5 = 25	4 × 1 = 4
2 × 1 = 2	4 × 2 = 8	3 × 4 = 12
	7 × 1 = 7	2 × 5 = 10

56 — Sprint: Multiplication from 1× to 9×
Target Time 2 / 3 / 4 min. · Date / / · Name

● Multiply.

7 × 9 = 63	2 × 3 = 6	1 × 2 = 2
1 × 4 = 4	8 × 9 = 72	8 × 4 = 32
6 × 2 = 12	5 × 7 = 35	5 × 1 = 5
2 × 7 = 14	4 × 3 = 12	9 × 7 = 63
3 × 9 = 27	7 × 5 = 35	4 × 5 = 20
9 × 1 = 9	3 × 1 = 3	6 × 4 = 24
8 × 3 = 24	6 × 6 = 36	2 × 6 = 12
4 × 8 = 32	4 × 7 = 28	3 × 7 = 21
6 × 7 = 42	9 × 8 = 72	7 × 3 = 21
3 × 5 = 15	1 × 6 = 6	4 × 9 = 36
6 × 5 = 30	5 × 9 = 54	9 × 6 = 54
7 × 4 = 28	2 × 9 = 18	1 × 1 = 1
2 × 2 = 4	3 × 3 = 9	5 × 8 = 40
1 × 5 = 5	8 × 1 = 8	8 × 7 = 56
9 × 3 = 27	7 × 8 = 56	9 × 8 = 54

Congratulations! You have really improved your speed and accuracy!

KUM◯N

Certificate of Achievement

is hereby congratulated on completing

Kumon Speed & Accuracy Math Workbook

Multiplication: Multiplying Numbers 1 Through 9

Presented on _____, 20____

_____
Parent or Guardian